LS IN TH   AN

THE ELEPHANT ARMY

AL-KISA
FOUNDATION
WWW.KISAKIDS.ORG

KISA KIDS
PUBLICATIONS

Long ago, there lived an evil king named Abraha. King Abraha dreamt of ruling the world. He wanted to be the greatest king ever! He didn't care who he hurt as long as he got what he wanted. So, Allah taught him a lesson that we all can learn from!

One day, King Abraha's soldiers told him about an amazing elephant that lived in the land of Habasha. This elephant was bigger and stronger than all other elephants in the world! When Abraha heard this, he said, "I have to have this elephant — no matter what it takes!" He ordered his soldiers to immediately go to Habasha and bring him this amazing elephant!

His soldiers did as they were told. Soon, they returned with the largest elephant anyone had ever seen! With every step the elephant took, the land would shake! It felt just like an earthquake!

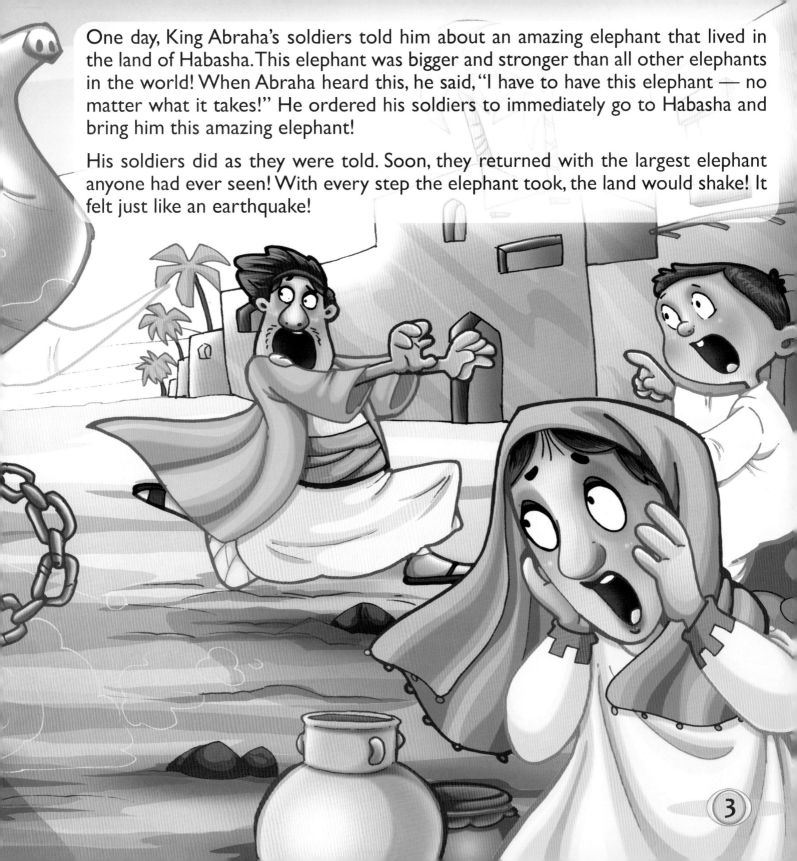

Abraha was jealous that everyone would go to the Holy Ka'bah in Mecca! You see, he didn't believe in Allah, and wanted people to worship him instead! So, he came up with a master plan. He was going to build an enormous temple! This way, everyone would come here to worship instead of going to the Ka'bah! But they didn't have large trucks back then. What was he going to do? So, he used the giant elephant to carry large rocks and tree trunks into the city.

It took two long months, but the temple was finally complete! The king named it Qalees and ordered his people to pray there instead of going to the Ka'bah. But his plan failed! No one came to Qalees, and everyone continued to worship at the Ka'bah! King Abraha became very angry! He thought: *How dare they not come to this temple!* So, he commanded his soldiers to prepare the army – they were going to destroy the Holy Ka'bah!

The army headed towards Mecca, with the powerful elephant leading the way. King Abraha wanted the elephant to destroy the Ka'bah once and for all! However, halfway to Mecca, the giant elephant suddenly stopped walking, sat on the ground, and refused to move forward.

"Maybe he's hungry! Let's get him some food!" one of the soldiers suggested. Another soldier ran and brought the best food they could find, but the elephant didn't eat a single bite!

"Maybe he is tired," the king suggested. "Let's stay here for the night and continue our journey tomorrow."

The next morning, the soldiers pulled on the elephant's rope to make him move, but he still did not budge!

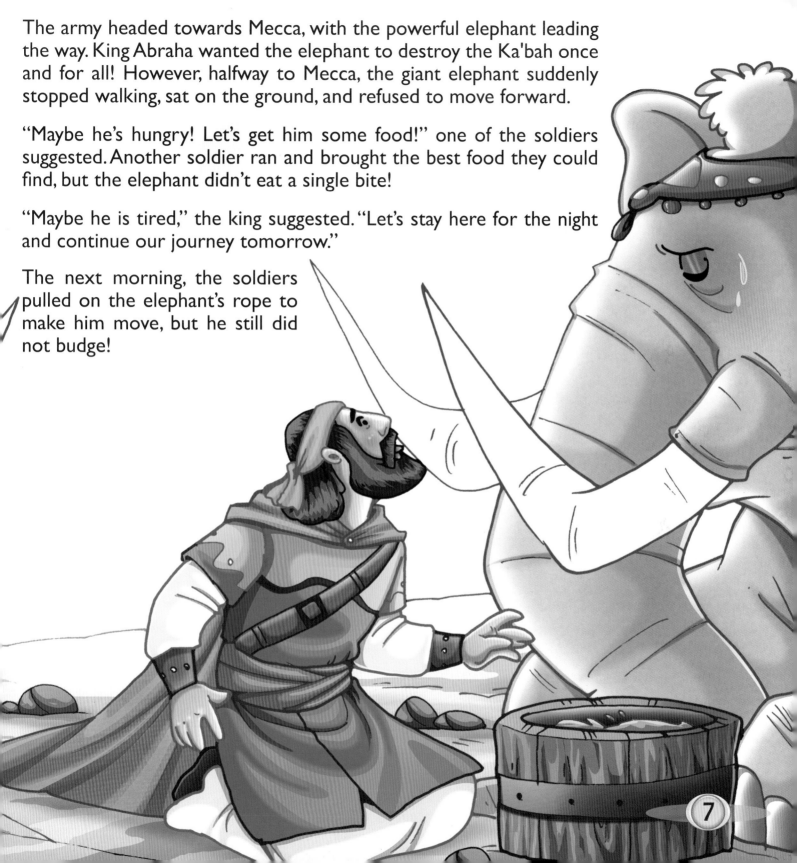

King Abraha couldn't take it anymore! He ordered his soldiers to whip the giant elephant so he would get up and walk. After the soldiers hurt him many times, the elephant sadly stood up again and continued marching towards the Ka'bah.

Soon, news spread all over Mecca that King Abraha was coming with an entire army to destroy the Ka'bah! The people quickly went to their leader, Abdul Mutallib, the grandfather of Prophet Muhammad (S).

Abdul Mutallib said confidently, "O people, don't worry! The God of the Ka'bah will protect it from the evil army." He also told the people to head into the mountains so they would be safe!

The next morning, the army arrived in Mecca and prepared to attack the Ka'bah. As they moved closer towards the Ka'bah, the giant elephant stopped moving again! It was almost like he knew the Ka'bah was holy! The soldiers began whipping the elephant again, but this time, it was of no use. The elephant refused to move forward even one step!

All of a sudden, they felt a huge shadow cast over their heads. They looked up and saw a huge flock of birds! Hidden in their beaks and claws were thousands of little stones. As they flew directly over the army, they dropped their stones, which rained down on the soldiers with great force!

Hundreds of the soldiers were killed by the the falling stones, and the rest ran away in fear. The great elephant also began to run and even trampled King Abraha under his large feet!

Through this story, we can learn a valuable lesson: no matter how big or small something may seem, Allah is the Most Powerful and the Best Protector! With His power, even the smallest stones can have the biggest effect!